the SCIENCE beHIND

TIME, TIDES, AND REVOLUTIONS

Nicolas Brasch

- ➲ What Causes the Seasons to Change?

- ➲ How Was Time Measured Before There Were Clocks?

- ➲ What Is the Difference between a Solar Eclipse and a Lunar Eclipse?

A⁺

Smart Apple Media
P.O. Box 3263
Mankato, MN, 56002

First published in 2010 by
MACMILLAN EDUCATION AUSTRALIA PTY LTD
15–19 Claremont St, South Yarra, Australia 3141

Visit our web site at www.macmillan.com.au or go directly to www.macmillanlibrary.com.au

Associated companies and representatives throughout the world.

Copyright © Nicolas Brasch 2010

Library of Congress Cataloging-in-Publication Data

Brasch, Nicolas.
    Times, tides, and revolutions / Nicolas Brasch.
        p. cm. — (The science behind)
    Includes index.
    ISBN 978-1-59920-563-2 (lib. bdg.)
    1. Earth—Rotation—Juvenile literature. 2. Time—Juvenile literature.
    3. Tides—Juvenile literature. I. Title.
    QB633.B735 2011
525'.35—dc22
                                                2009045109

Publisher: Carmel Heron
Managing Editor: Vanessa Lanaway
Editor: Georgina Garner
Proofreader: Kylie Cockle
Designer: Stella Vassiliou
Page layout: Stella Vassiliou and Raul Diche
Photo researcher: Sarah Johnson
Illustrators: Map on page 23 courtesy of Geo Atlas, modified by Raul Diche; Alan Laver, pp. 24, 26, 27 (top), 28; Richard Morden, p. 8; Melissa Webb, pp. 10, 11, 12, 14, 27 (bottom), 29, 30, 31; Karen Young, p. 1.
Production Controller: Vanessa Johnson

Manufactured in China by Macmillan Production (Asia) Ltd.
Kwun Tong, Kowloon, Hong Kong
Supplier Code: CP December 2009

Acknowledgments
The author and the publisher are grateful to the following for permission to reproduce copyright material:

Front cover photograph:
Red alarm clock, © Baris Simsek/iStockphoto; Full moon, © Oliver911119/Shutterstock; Earth, © National Aeronautics and Space Administration (NASA).

Photos courtesy of:
The Art Archive/Bodleian Library Oxford, **22**; The Art Archive/Pharaonic Village Cairo/Gianni Dagli Orti, **19** (top); Australian War Memorial Negative Number REL/07581.001, **21** (middle); Image © de:Benutzer:Flyout, http://en.wikipedia.org/wiki/File:Kerzenuhr.jpg, **19** (bottom); Getty Images, **9** (left & right), **31** (top); Popperfoto/Getty Images, **7** (right); © DNY59/iStockphoto, **19** (middle); © Tobias Helbig/iStockphoto, **31** (middle); © Sven Klaschik/iStockphoto, **4**; © Paolo Gaetano Rocco/iStockphoto, **15** (top); © wsfurlan/iStockphoto, **20** (right); Jupiter Unlimited, **7** (left); Library of Congress Vatican Exhibit, **8**; National Aeronautics Space Administration (NASA), **6** (top); Image courtesy National Institute of Standards and Technology (NIST), **20** (left), **21** (bottom); © National Maritime Museum, Greenwich, London, **21** (top); Karan Kapoor/Photolibrary, **13** (bottom); Antonello Lanzellotto/Photolibrary, **18** (bottom); Reuters/Bobby Yip, **5**; © Andre Blais/Shutterstock, **25** (right); © Matthew Jacques/Shutterstock, **6** (bottom); © Zastol'skiy Victor Leonidovich/Shutterstock, **16**; © Oliver911119/Shutterstock, **15** (top); © Vakhrushev Pavel/Shutterstock, **13** (top); © Spauln/Shutterstock, **17**; © Ekaterina Starshaya/Shutterstock, **30** (top); © Supri Suharjoto/Shutterstock, **25** (left).

While every care has been taken to trace and acknowledge copyright, the publisher tenders their apologies for any accidental infringement where copyright has proved untraceable. Where the attempt has been unsuccessful, the publisher welcomes information that would redress the situation.

The publisher would like to thank Heidi Ruhnau, Head of Science at Oxley College, for her assistance in reviewing manuscripts.

Please note
At the time of printing, the Internet addresses appearing in this book were correct. Owing to the dynamic nature of the Internet, however, we cannot guarantee that all these addresses will remain correct.

▶ Contents

Look out for these features throughout the book:

"Word Watch" explains the meanings of words shown in **bold**

"Web Watch" provides web site suggestions for further research

Understanding the World Through Science

Science = Knowledge
The word *"science"* comes from the Latin word *scientia,* which means "knowledge."

▲ Humans look at the things around them and ask "Why?" and "How?" Science helps answer these questions.

Science is amazing! Through science, people can understand more about the world and themselves. Without science, humans would not have a clue—about anything!

Shared Knowledge

Science exists because humans are curious. They are curious about how things work, about Earth and its place in the universe, about life and survival, about the natural world around them, and about time, space, and speed. They are curious about everything! They never stop asking questions.

Science is the knowledge that humans have gathered about the physical and natural world and how it works. This knowledge is gathered through **experimentation** and **observation**.

The Science Behind Time, Tides, and Revolutions

For thousands of years, humans have used observation, experimentation, and **calculation** to determine how and why the sun, Moon, and planets seem to move around the sky. Humans have also determined how time should be measured and named.

Humans could not change the **phenomena** of tides and revolutions, but they wanted to study them and understand them. Since ancient times, many theories have been put forward and many discoveries made. Scientists have determined how gravity works and how the planets and the moons affect one another.

Humans could not change the amount of light and dark that occurred each day, either, but once they understood these regular movements, they could measure them and name them. Humans put 24 hours in the day, 60 minutes in the hour, and 60 seconds in the minute. They invented clocks, daylight saving time, and the International Date Line.

Time, Tide, and Revolution Scientists

Different types of scientists study time, tides, and revolutions.

Scientist and Area of Study

Astronomer Planets, stars, and other bodies in the skies

Physicist Time, motion, energy, and other natural phenomena

Astrophysicist How light, motion, and other natural phenomena act with bodies in the universe

Astrobiologist Origin of life on Earth and the possibility of life on other planets

Oceanographer Tides, currents, waves, and other features of the oceans

▲ Many curious humans have watched and wondered about the changing night sky.

Word Watch

calculation using mathematics to determine the size or number of something

phenomena happenings or occurrences

5

Why Did People Once Think that Earth Was Flat?

Long ago, most civilizations thought that Earth was flat. It wasn't until the ancient Greeks began to use science and mathematics to make discoveries about Earth that people began to question this belief.

▲ Images taken from satellites in space show us that Earth is a sphere.

A Reasonable Assumption

While the idea that Earth is flat seems ridiculous now that we have photographs from space showing that Earth is a **sphere**, such an **assumption** was not so ridiculous several thousand years ago. People came to the conclusion that Earth was flat after observing the land around them. They were not able to travel vast distances across the land, as we do today. Instead, they observed the land near their homes and concluded that as far as the land reached, it was flat. It certainly did not appear curved, like a sphere.

Word Watch

assumption thing that is accepted as true, but without proof

sphere round, three-dimensional object where all points on the surface are the same distance from the center

▲ If you observe the small area of land around your home, as people in ancient times did, Earth appears flat.

The Ancient Greeks Provide Proof

There was no single mathematician or scientist who suddenly announced that Earth was a sphere. Instead, between 600 B.C. and 200 B.C., many scientists and mathematicians from Greece used different methods to come to similar conclusions.

Pythagoras (580–500 B.C.) observed that all the bodies in space appear to be spheres and that, therefore, Earth must be a sphere as well. Aristotle (384–322 B.C.) noted how the stars appear to rise in the distance and concluded that their appearance this way could not occur if Earth were flat. About 100 years later, Eratosthenes (275–194 B.C.) noted that the shadows cast by the sun at midday in two different cities were of very different lengths. This would not be the case if Earth were flat. Eratosthenes used this information to calculate the **circumference** of Earth.

The Columbus Myth

Christopher Columbus (1451–1506) sailed across the Atlantic Ocean in 1492 searching for Asia. Some history books record that members of his crew were concerned that they might sail over the edge of the world. This myth is untrue. By 1492, it had long been accepted that Earth was a sphere.

Religion and a Flat Earth

When scientists and mathematicians began to prove that Earth was a sphere, some religious leaders remained firm that Earth was flat. A flat Earth helped explain how "heaven" could be physically above Earth and "hell" physically below it.

◄ Aristotle was a philosopher, teacher, and scientist whose thoughts and ideas helped form modern Western civilization.

▲ The explorer Christopher Columbus knew Earth was not flat. He thought he would come to Asia if he sailed west across the Atlantic Ocean, but instead he came to the Americas.

Word Watch

circumference
distance around the outside of a circle or sphere

How Did We Work Out that Earth Revolves Around the Sun?

The first person to determine that Earth revolves around the sun was the Greek astronomer and mathematician Aristarchus. Many later astronomers agreed, but most people did not believe it until Galileo Galilei and his telescope proved the **theory**.

Aristarchus's Calculations

When Aristarchus (around 310–230 B.C.) observed the shadow that Earth made on the Moon during a lunar **eclipse** (see pages 30–31), he first began to consider the possibility that Earth revolved around the sun. He made **calculations** and models and, putting all his findings together, he concluded that the sun was at the center of the planets and everything revolved around the sun, not Earth.

Standing on Earth and looking up, it appears as if the sun is moving across the sky and Earth is standing still. Aristarchus argued that Earth was moving on its **axis**, which resulted in it appearing as if the sun was revolving around Earth. He was right, but he could not prove it. People preferred to trust their own eyes.

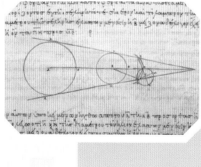

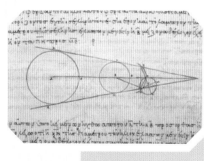

◀ Aristarchus made complicated calculations about the size of the sun, Earth, and Moon. He was trying to prove that Earth revolves around the sun.

Midday

8:00 A.M.

4:00 P.M.

▲ In the past, people thought that the sun revolved around Earth. This was because the sun appears to move across the sky during the day.

Ptolemy's Model

Another important Greek astronomer was Ptolemy (around A.D. 85–165). Ptolemy believed that Earth was a fixed, central body, with all the planets and the sun revolving around Earth. He published calculations, drawings, and models to try to prove his point, in a work called *Almagest*. His view was so respected that it was not questioned.

Copernicus's Work

Polish astronomer Nicolaus Copernicus (1473–1543) examined Ptolemy's work and found that it just did not match what seemed to be happening in the skies, no matter how the calculations were fiddled with. He concluded that these differences could easily be explained if Earth was moving.

Copernicus's views were not accepted, because his model went against the Catholic Church's beliefs. After the invention of the telescope, however, **observations** by Italian astronomer Galileo Galilei (1564–1692) proved that Copernicus was correct and Earth does revolve around the sun.

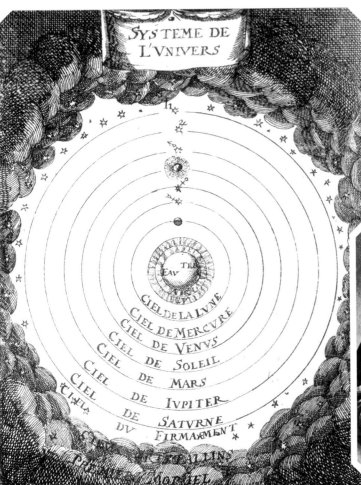

◀ Ptolemy's model shows the sun and the planets revolving around Earth.

▼ Copernicus worked on his theory for more than 30 years and it was published just before his death.

The Catholic Church and Heliocentrism

The Catholic Church was the dominant force in Europe during the time of Copernicus and Galileo. The Church believed that humans were the center of the universe and parts of the Bible say that Earth could not be moved. The Church disagreed with Copernicus's work and in 1633, Galileo was charged with **heresy** for following the work of Copernicus.

Word Watch

heresy belief or opinion that goes against religious belief

observations information that is gained by watching something carefully

Web Watch

sunearthday.nasa.gov/2006/locations/ptolemy.php

sunearthday.nasa.gov/2006/locations/greece.php

How Long Does It Take for Earth to Orbit the Sun?

It takes 365 days, 5 hours, 48 minutes, and 46 seconds (or 365.242 days) for Earth to **orbit** the sun. If that length of time looks familiar, it is because it is just more than one year.

Yearly Orbit

Earth follows the same path in its orbit around the sun each year. Earth's orbit around the sun, however, does not take exactly 365 days. It takes almost six hours longer. In order to keep the yearly calendar in line with Earth's progress around the sun, an extra day is added in some years, called leap years.

Keeping the Seasons in the Right Months

Without the extra day in leap years, the timing of seasons would change over hundreds of years. January and February are winter months in the northern hemisphere and summer months in the southern hemisphere. Without leap years, over time, these months would experience different seasons.

▼ Earth travels 92,960,000 miles (149,600,000 km) in its orbit around the sun.

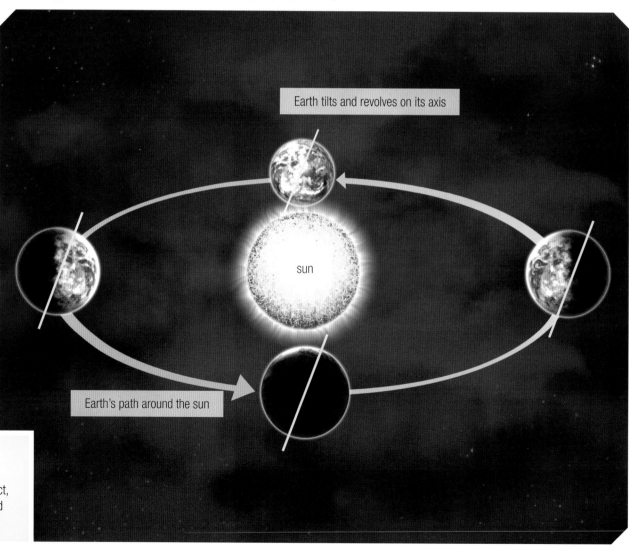

Earth tilts and revolves on its axis

sun

Earth's path around the sun

Leap Years

In a leap year, there are 29 days in February, instead of 28 days as in other years. This means there are 366 days in a leap year, instead of 365.

A leap year occurs every four years. It takes almost six hours more than 365 days for Earth to orbit the sun. If you multiply that six hours by four, which is the **frequency** of leap years, you get the extra day needed to keep everything running together. There is still a slight difference, however, that has to be accounted for, so some leap years are kept as normal 365-day years. If a year is evenly divisible by 100 and not also evenly divisible by 400, a leap year is not held. So, 2000 was a leap year, as 2400 will be, but 2100, 2200, and 2300 will not be leap years.

Night and Day

While Earth orbits the sun, it also turns on its **axis**, spinning around. The time it takes for Earth to spin all the way around is what we call a day. As Earth spins, the part of Earth facing the sun changes. This is how we get day and night.

Solar Year

The sun has a year, too. The sun orbits the Milky Way galaxy. It is thought that it takes more than 200 million Earth years to orbit it once. If anyone lived on the sun, they would celebrate their birthday just once every 200 million Earth years.

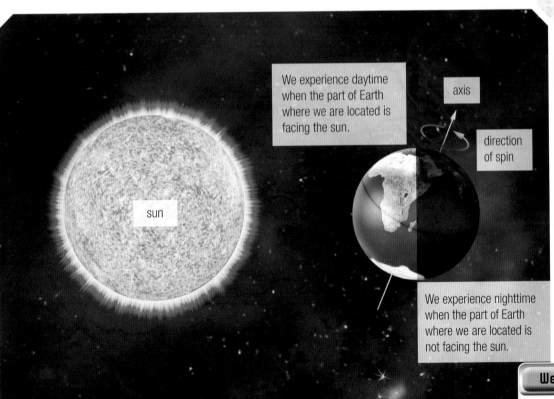

We experience daytime when the part of Earth where we are located is facing the sun.

axis

direction of spin

sun

We experience nighttime when the part of Earth where we are located is not facing the sun.

▲ During its yearly orbit, Earth also spins on its axis, creating day and night.

Word **W**atch

axis imaginary line around which something, such as Earth, spins

frequency number of times something occurs in a given time period

Web Watch ▼

www.enchantedlearning.com/subjects/astronomy/planets/earth/

What Causes the Seasons to Change?

As Earth **orbits** the sun, it spins on its **axis**. Earth is tilted at an angle to its own path. It is this tilt that creates the different seasons.

The Tilt of Earth

Earth is tilted at an angle of 23.45 degrees. This means that parts of Earth tilt toward the sun at certain times of the year and tilt away from the sun at other times of the year. The degree of the tilt never changes. It is Earth's position in relation to the sun that changes. This creates the seasons.

Some people believe that the seasons occur because parts of Earth are closer to the sun than others at times, but this is not true. It is the angle at which sunlight hits Earth that determines the seasons.

▼ During a hemisphere's summer, sunlight hits that hemisphere directly. During a hemisphere's winter, sunlight hits the area on an angle, so it is less strong.

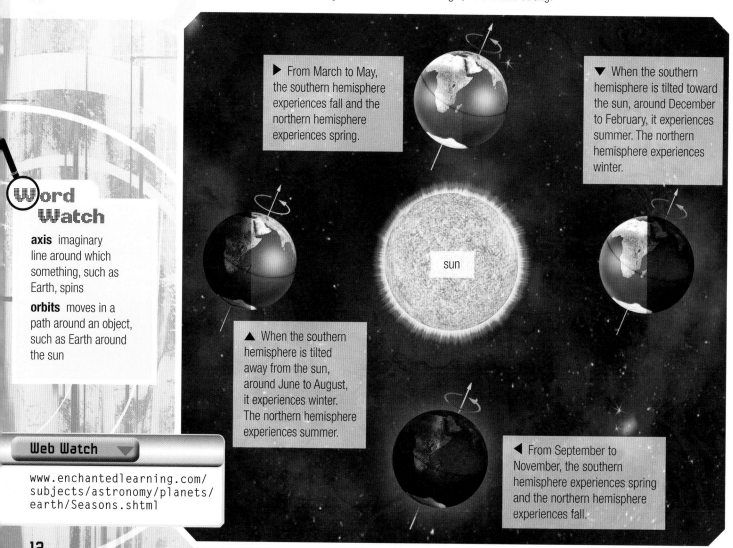

▶ From March to May, the southern hemisphere experiences fall and the northern hemisphere experiences spring.

▼ When the southern hemisphere is tilted toward the sun, around December to February, it experiences summer. The northern hemisphere experiences winter.

sun

▲ When the southern hemisphere is tilted away from the sun, around June to August, it experiences winter. The northern hemisphere experiences summer.

◀ From September to November, the southern hemisphere experiences spring and the northern hemisphere experiences fall.

Summer and Winter

Summer occurs when the northern or southern hemisphere is tilted toward the sun. Winter occurs when either is tilted away from the sun. During the summer, the sun is higher in the sky, its rays hit the ground more directly, and the days are longer.

Spring and Fall

During the spring, the amount and degree of sunlight in a hemisphere begins to increase as the hemisphere emerges from winter. Plants begin to grow and flower, as they start receiving nourishment from the sunlight, which they were deprived of for several months. During the fall, the reverse happens. The position of Earth changes and less and less sunlight gets through.

Solstices

Solstices are days when Earth is positioned in such a way that the hemispheres receive the most or the least amount of daily sunlight in the year. One solstice occurs on December 21 or 22, and another on June 20 or 21.

Equinoxes

Equinoxes occur twice a year when Earth is positioned in such a way that its tilt is neither angled toward or away from the sun. The day and the night are of equal length. One equinox occurs on March 20 or 21, and another on September 22 or 23.

▲ During the summer, the land is tilted toward the sun so the weather is warmer.

Web Watch ▼

www.bbc.co.uk/science/space/solarsystem/earth/solsticescience.shtml

Why Are There 12 Months in a Year?

The ancient Romans introduced a calendar that had 12 months in the year. The length of a month roughly equals the length of synodic and sidereal months, which measure the movement of the Moon around Earth.

Synodic Months and Sidereal Months

The time that it takes for the Moon to go through all its phases is called a synodic month or lunar month. These phases are determined by the amount of sunlight that can be seen on the Moon. A synodic month is 29.531 days.

The time that it takes for the Moon to **orbit** Earth once is called a sidereal month. A sidereal month is 27.322 days.

Calendar months were based on synodic and sidereal months. Earth's year of 365 or 366 days was divided into months of 28, 29, 30, or 31 days. Twelve months fit in one year.

Observing the Moon's Changes

Ancient civilizations used synodic months in their calendars because they were easy to calculate. All they had to do was look up at the Moon. They did not have the equipment or the knowledge to calculate the exact time it took for the Moon to orbit Earth.

Word Watch

orbit move in a path around an object, such as Earth around the sun

Web Watch

www.sumanasinc.com/
webcontent/animations/
content/sidereal.html

www.calendar-origins.
com/calendar-name-
origins.html

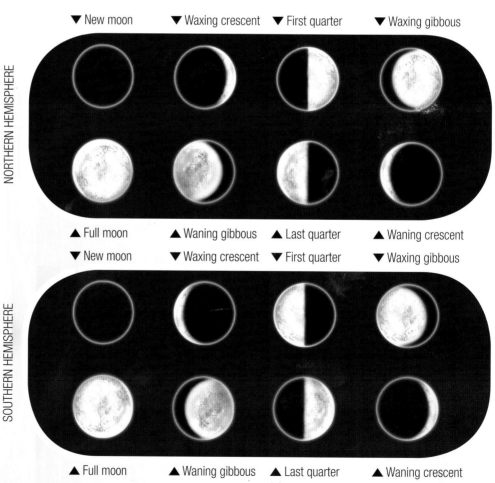

NORTHERN HEMISPHERE

▼ New moon   ▼ Waxing crescent   ▼ First quarter   ▼ Waxing gibbous

▲ Full moon   ▲ Waning gibbous   ▲ Last quarter   ▲ Waning crescent

SOUTHERN HEMISPHERE

▼ New moon   ▼ Waxing crescent   ▼ First quarter   ▼ Waxing gibbous

▲ Full moon   ▲ Waning gibbous   ▲ Last quarter   ▲ Waning crescent

▲ The Moon's phases appear differently, depending on whether you are seeing them from the northern hemisphere or the southern hemisphere.

▲ The ancient Romans divided the year into 12 months. Each month related to the movement and the phases of the Moon.

Names of the Months

The English names of our months come from the months in ancient Roman calendars.

Month	Origin of Name
January	Named after Janus, the Roman god of doorways and beginnings
February	Named after the Roman festival of Februa, which was the feast of **purification**
March	Named after Mars, the Roman god of war
April	Originally called Aprilis by the Romans and probably named after the Greek goddess of love, Aphrodite
May	Named after Maia, the Greek goddess of spring
June	Named after Juno, the Roman goddess of marriage and women
July	Named after the Roman emperor Julius Caesar
August	Named after the Roman emperor Augustus
September	From *septem*, the Latin word for seven (originally the seventh month)
October	From *octo*, the Latin word for eight (originally the eighth month)
November	From *novem*, the Latin word for nine (originally the ninth month)
December	From *decem*, the Latin word for 10 (originally the tenth month)

Caesar's Leap Years

The idea to add an extra day to February every four years came from the astronomer Sosigenes of Alexandria. Sosigenes was ordered by Julius Caesar (100–44 B.C.), Emperor of Rome, to work out how to align the days and months with the length of a year.

▲ Roman emperor Julius Caesar introduced the Julian calendar and its 12 months in 46 B.C.

Word Watch

purification process of getting rid of unhealthy materials such as from one's body and unhealthy thoughts from one's mind

Why Are There 24 Hours in a Day?

A day is the time it takes Earth to move all the way around on its **axis**. It was the ancient Sumerians and Babylonians who decided to divide this natural period into 24 equal units, called hours.

Sidereal Days and Solar Days

As Earth turns on its axis, the view in the sky changes. At nighttime, in darkness, the most obvious change is the position of the stars. By pinpointing the position of a star in the sky and then checking when the star is next in that exact position, one day can be measured. A day measured in this way is known as a sidereal day. A sidereal day is 23 hours, 56 minutes, and 4.1 seconds long.

Another way of measuring a day is to pinpoint when the sun is directly overhead. The next time it is directly overhead marks the passing of one day. A day measured in this way is known as a solar day. A solar day is exactly 24 hours long.

Difference in Length of Sidereal and Solar Days

The difference in the length of sidereal and solar days is because Earth is turning on its axis as well as **orbiting** the sun. It has to turn a tiny bit more for the sun to appear in the same spot as the day before, so a solar day is about four minutes longer than a sidereal day.

Word Watch

axis imaginary line around which something, such as Earth, spins

orbiting moving in a path around an object, such as Earth around the sun

Web Watch

scienceworld.wolfram.com/astronomy/SiderealDay.html

▲ A star appears in the same position in the night sky every 23 hours, 56 minutes, and 4.1 seconds. Like the sun seems to move across the sky during the day, the stars seem to move across the sky during the night.

The Sumerians and Babylonians

The Sumerians and Babylonians lived in Mesopotamia, in southwestern Asia, where Iraq is today. The Sumerians were the dominant civilization in the area from about 3500 B.C. until 2000 B.C., when the Babylonians took over. It was the Sumerians and Babylonians who invented hours, dividing a day into 24 equal-sized periods.

Base 60 System

Both of these civilizations used a base 60 system in their mathematics. This means that they used 60 different numerals, rather than just 10 different numerals (1–10) like we use today. They divided each hour into 60 minutes and each minute into 60 seconds.

It is not certain why the Sumerians and Babylonians divided the day into 24 hours. One **theory** is that the Babylonians first divided a day into two parts of 12 hours each, one part for the daylight hours and one part for the night. They used the number 12 because the four fingers (ignoring the thumb) on a hand have three segments, making 12 different segments. Adding the 12 from one hand to the 12 on the other hand equals 24. This could also explain why the Sumerians and Babylonians used base 60. Multiplying the number of finger segments on one hand (12) by the number of fingers on the other hand (5) equals 60.

Days of the Week

- ⊃ Sunday means day of the sun.
- ⊃ Monday means day of the Moon.
- ⊃ Tuesday is named after Tyr, a **Norse** god.
- ⊃ Wednesday is named after Woden, or Odin, a **Germanic** god.
- ⊃ Thursday is named after Thor, a Norse god.
- ⊃ Friday is named after Frige, a Germanic goddess.
- ⊃ Saturday is named after Saturn, a Roman god.

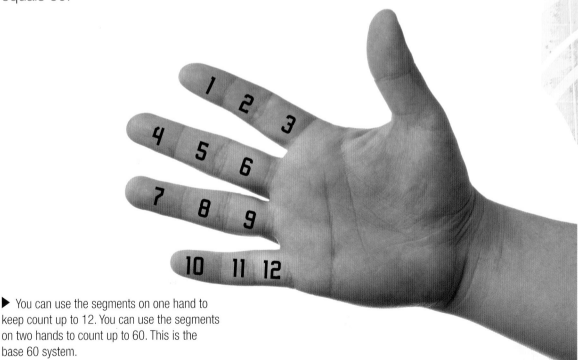

▶ You can use the segments on one hand to keep count up to 12. You can use the segments on two hands to count up to 60. This is the base 60 system.

Word Watch

Germanic relating to the ancient people of northern and western Europe

Norse relating to the people of the Scandinavian countries of Sweden, Norway, Denmark, Finland, and Iceland

theory an idea used to explain something

How Was Time Measured Before There Were Clocks?

Throughout history, humans have created many devices to measure time. These devices have included sundials, sandglasses, water clocks, and candles.

Sundials

Many civilizations have used sundials to tell the time. The oldest surviving sundials date back to the Egyptians in 1500 B.C. In ancient writings, there is mention of sundials dating back a further 2,000 years.

Sundials work by placing an object on a clear area of ground, where sunlight can reach it clearly without being blocked by buildings, trees, or other large objects. When a sundial is first set up, markings are made on the ground to indicate the passing of time. Once marked, people can check where the shadow of the sundial is pointing and see what time it is.

Sundials made it possible to set meeting times in the same way that people today say, "Let's meet at 11 o'clock tomorrow morning." Sundials have one major setback, however. Time cannot be recorded at night because there is no sunlight to cast a shadow.

Obelisk of Montecitorio

The **Obelisk** of Montecitorio is a 72-feet- (22-m-) high stone structure in Rome, in Italy. It originally stood in Egypt but it was taken to Rome in 10 B.C. by Emperor Augustus (63 B.C. – A.D. 14). It operates as a sundial. A shadow originating from the top of the obelisk is cast on markings in the square where it stands.

The sundial reads 10: A.M.

10 11 12 3 4 5 6 9 8 7 6

A.M. P.M. Standard time

Word Watch

obelisk tall, four-sided stone pillar that has a pyramid at the top

▲ Wood and stone were the most common materials for sundials.

Web Watch

www.egipto.
com/obeliscos/
montecitorio2.html

▶ The Obelisk of Montecitorio is an Egyptian sundial that stands in Piazza Montecitorio in Rome, in Italy.

Water Clocks

Water clocks were invented because sundials could not be used to tell the time at night or on cloudy days. Water clocks measure drips.

Originally, a water clock was a large pot with a small hole at the bottom. Markings to indicate intervals of time were engraved on the side of the pot. As the water dripped out, people could tell the time of day by noting the point that the water level reached.

There were several problems with water clocks:

- ⮑ to tell the time, a person needed to know when the pot was last filled up
- ⮑ someone had to remember to fill the water clock when it was empty
- ⮑ in very cold weather, the water would freeze

Sandglasses

Sandglasses work in a similar way to water clocks, except that time is measured by the movement of sand, not water. A sandglass is also known as an hourglass.

A sandglass consists of two bulbs joined together but separated by a tiny hole. The sandglass is turned and sand trickles down from the bulb on top. When all the sand has passed into the bottom bulb, a certain period of time has passed.

Candles

Candles have also been used to measure the passing of time. Marks are engraved into them. As the candle burns down to each mark, another period of time has passed.

▲ As the water drained slowly out, the marks on the inside of this ancient Egyptian water clock would show the time.

▶ As the candle burns down, the time can be calculated using marks beside the candle.

Sandglasses Today

Sandglasses were first used by sailors more than 1,000 years ago to mark the passing of time at sea. They are often used today to measure time limits for certain tasks, such as boiling an egg or taking a shower.

Measuring Time— But Not Telling the Time

Water clocks, sandglasses, and candles have one major drawback. While they measure the passing of time, they do not indicate what time it is!

▶ A sandglass measures a certain period of time.

Web Watch ▼

www.tkyoung.com/history.html

How Accurate Is the Most Accurate Clock on Earth?

Since the 1950s, the world's most accurate clocks have been atomic clocks. Some atomic clocks that are being developed have been recorded as having an accuracy level of one second in 200 million years. This means they will lose only one second in time every 200 million years.

Minerals in Clocks

The most accurate atomic clocks being developed use atoms from the metals aluminum and mercury. Quartz crystals are also used to measure time. Most modern clocks and watches use quartz technology.

Measuring Motion

Atomic clocks use the vibrations of **atoms** to record time. Before they were invented, time was measured by the swinging of a **pendulum**. The faster the motion, the more accurate the clock. The pendulum in most grandfather clocks swings once every second. In contrast, the atoms in the latest atomic clocks vibrate at a rate of billions of times every second. Grandfather clocks need to be wound up weekly or even daily so they keep going, but an atomic clock could be left for billions of years and still be very accurate.

◀ A grandfather clock measures time by the swinging of its pendulum. The pendulum is protected in the wooden body of the clock.

▲ This atomic clock is currently used as the official standard for measuring time in the United States. It is accurate to about one second in 30 million years.

Word Watch

atoms the smallest particles of matter, which make up everything in the world

pendulum weighted piece of wire, rope, or other material that swings at a regular rate

Web Watch

whyfiles.org/078time/

Timeline of Clocks

Before **mechanical** clocks, people used sundials, water clocks, sandglasses, and candles to measure time (see pages 18–19). Since around A.D. 1400, many types of mechanical clock have been used.

Word Watch

mechanical working as a machine

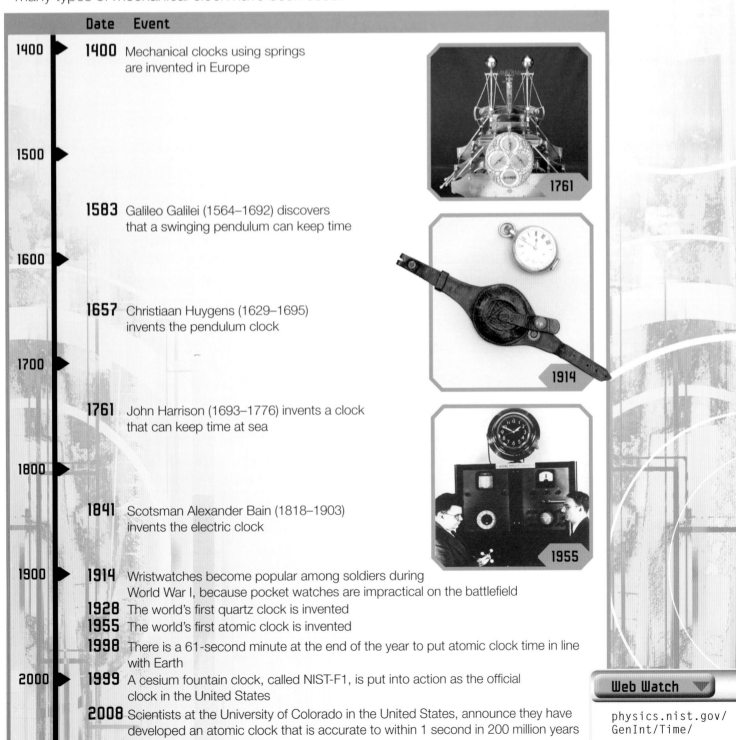

Date	Event
1400	Mechanical clocks using springs are invented in Europe
1583	Galileo Galilei (1564–1692) discovers that a swinging pendulum can keep time
1657	Christiaan Huygens (1629–1695) invents the pendulum clock
1761	John Harrison (1693–1776) invents a clock that can keep time at sea
1841	Scotsman Alexander Bain (1818–1903) invents the electric clock
1914	Wristwatches become popular among soldiers during World War I, because pocket watches are impractical on the battlefield
1928	The world's first quartz clock is invented
1955	The world's first atomic clock is invented
1998	There is a 61-second minute at the end of the year to put atomic clock time in line with Earth
1999	A cesium fountain clock, called NIST-F1, is put into action as the official clock in the United States
2008	Scientists at the University of Colorado in the United States, announce they have developed an atomic clock that is accurate to within 1 second in 200 million years

Image labels: 1761, 1914, 1955

Web Watch

physics.nist.gov/GenInt/Time/

What Is the International Date Line?

The International Date Line is an imaginary line that passes through the Pacific Ocean in a north–south direction. Countries immediately to the west of the line are a day ahead of countries immediately to the east of it.

The Need for the Date Line

Going Back in Time?

If a person flies from Wellington, in New Zealand, to Los Angeles, in the United States, they might leave at 6:30 A.M. Monday and arrive at 11:30 P.M. Sunday, the night before they left! They have not gone back in time. They have just passed the International Date Line.

The creation of the International Date Line in 1884 solved a problem that was known as the circumnavigator's paradox. When humans started traveling long distances from their homes, it became clear that there was a problem keeping time. This was particularly the case on long sea voyages.

If a ship left port at 6:00 P.M. and sailed swiftly westward, in the same direction as the sun appeared to be passing across the sky, it would most likely still be light four hours later. So while it was obviously 10:00 P.M. back at port, it could not be 10:00 P.M. on the ship because there was still daylight.

If the ship went on a very long voyage, either eastward or westward, it would eventually lose or gain a day. The first record of this happening is from 1522, when a crew member who accompanied Ferdinand Magellan (1480–1521) in the first circumnavigation around the world returned to find that it was Thursday in Portugal and not Wednesday as his records said it would be.

◀ When the Portuguese explorer Magellan sailed around the world in the 1500s, the circumnavigator's paradox became obvious. This map shows Magellan's ship sailing across the Pacific Ocean.

The Path of the Date Line

The International Date Line is not a straight line. If it was, it would pass right through the middle of some countries and it would be one day on one side of the country and a completely different day on the other side. Instead, the date line is drawn around some island countries rather than through them.

Time Zones

The International Date Line is not the only imaginary line that extends across Earth in a north–south direction. Twenty-four imaginary lines divide Earth into 24 different time zones.

The starting point for the time zones is in Greenwich, in England. The line that passes through Greenwich is called 0 degrees longitude and the International Date Line is on the other side of Earth at 180 degrees. There are 15 degrees between each of the other lines. The 15-degree difference represents 1/24 of Earth and each section represents one hour of time.

Creating Local Time

Sandford Fleming (1827–1915) was a Scottish-born Canadian engineer who came up with the idea for time zones in the late 1870s after becoming frustrated with train timetables while traveling. Before then, there was no consistency in time-keeping in nearby countries and even cities.

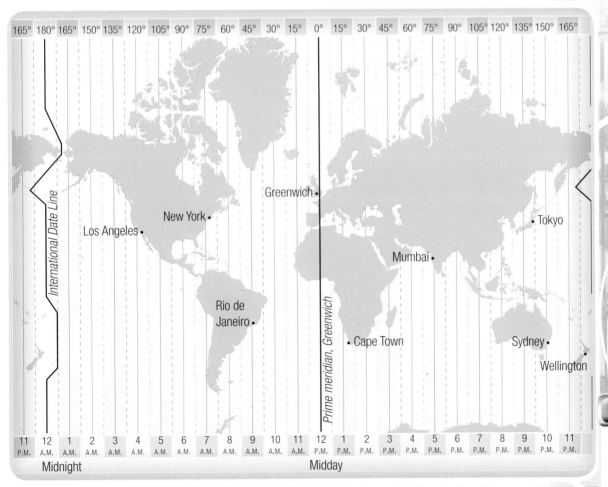

Web Watch

geography.
about.com/od/
physicalgeography/
a/idl.htm

▲ When it is midday in Greenwich, in England, it is usually 10:00 P.M. in Sydney and 7:00 A.M. in New York.

Why Do Some Places Use Daylight Saving Time?

Daylight saving time allows communities to have an extra hour of light in the afternoon or evening, while they are awake to enjoy it. This is not an extra hour of sunlight. This hour has just been taken from early in the morning when most people are asleep.

A Sunny Idea

William Willett (1857–1915) was a British builder who came up with the idea for daylight saving time in 1907, after noticing that many houses had their blinds drawn in the early evening. Daylight saving time was introduced by the British Parliament in 1916.

How Does Daylight Saving Time Work?

During their spring time, states and countries around the world that use daylight saving time put their clocks forward by one hour. This means that 5:00 P.M. normal time, according to the position of the sun, become 6:00 P.M. daylight saving time. This gives communities an extra hour of sunlight in the evening. At the beginning of the day, however, 5:00 A.M. according to the sun becomes 6:00 A.M., so it is dark for later in the mornings. At the end of summer, the clocks are put back to normal time.

▶ Countries that are far north or south of the equator are more likely to use daylight saving time. Countries near the equator have almost equal amounts of day and night all year round, so they do not need daylight saving time.

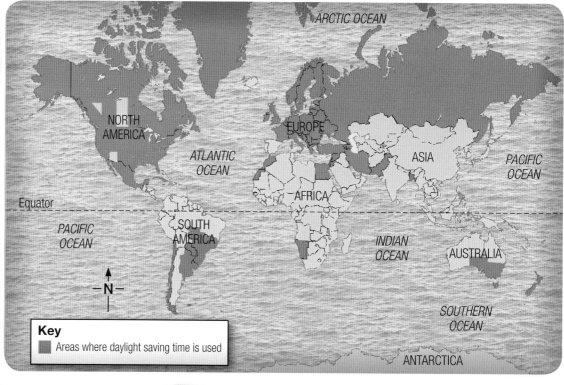

Key
  Areas where daylight saving time is used

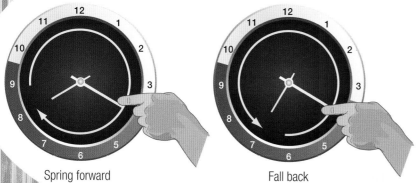

Spring forward

Fall back

◀ One way to remember when to turn the clock forward and when to turn it back is to remember the saying "Spring forward, fall back." When people crouch down and then spring up, they spring forward. So the clock goes forward in spring. When people fall, they generally fall backward and the clock also goes backward in fall.

For and Against

Daylight saving time has always had both supporters and opponents. William Willett was a supporter. Some dairy farmers today are opponents.

Arguments For Daylight Saving Time

✓ Supporters of daylight saving time say that one major advantage is that it saves energy. During the 1970s, when the United States suffered an oil shortage, President Jimmy Carter (1924–) extended daylight saving time to save on oil used for heating and lighting.

✓ Supporters argue that daylight saving is good for retail businesses because people have more daylight shopping hours.

✓ Supporters argue that motor vehicle accidents are reduced, because people driving home from work are more likely to be driving in daylight than in darkness.

Arguments Against Daylight Saving Time

✗ Many people who are opposed to daylight saving are farmers. Animals' activities are largely driven by sunlight, so farmers have to change the times they carry out some tasks, even though others do not change. Cows that were milked at 6:00 A.M. when the sun rises now have to be milked at 7:00 A.M. when the sun rises—but if the milk truck is still due at 11:00 A.M., the farmer loses an hour of work time in the morning.

✗ It can also be very confusing in countries where some states use daylight saving time and others do not, or in areas where neighboring countries have a time difference because of daylight saving.

Changing the Time

Daylight saving time usually starts and finishes at 2:00 A.M. on a Sunday morning. This time causes the least amount of inconvenience and confusion, because most people are asleep and most businesses are closed.

Saving Energy During Wartime

Daylight saving was first introduced during World War I so that people did not sleep through valuable daylight hours early in the morning and require artificial lighting to work or read in the late afternoon. During World War I and World War II, several countries extended their number of daylight saving hours to more than one hour.

▲ Supporters of daylight saving time argue that people are more likely to shop in daylight hours.

▲ Some people opposed to daylight saving time argue that it makes life harder for dairy farmers.

Web Watch

www.webexhibits.org/daylightsaving/

Why Don't We Fall Off the Face of Earth?

Earth is a **sphere** revolving in space, but no one falls off it. Humans and all other objects do not fall off the face of Earth because of **gravity**.

What Is Gravity?

Gravity is the **force** that exists between things that have **mass**. Any object that is close enough to another will try and pull the other object toward them.

The strength of the force of gravity is not equal for every object. The more mass an object has, the stronger its force of gravity will be. If a small object is placed near a large object, the small object will attempt to pull the other object toward it, but the gravitational pull of the larger object is more powerful. The larger object will drag the smaller object toward it.

Only the force of gravity from a gigantic object, such as Earth, can be noticed and felt. Everything on Earth is pulled toward the center of Earth.

Earth's Pull

The strength of Earth's gravitational force is 32.15 feet (9.8 m) per second per second. If an object is falling, it will increase its speed by 32.15 feet (9.8 m) every second—as long it is not slowed down by air resistance. The mass of an object does not change the rate of fall. In other words, a brick and a pencil that are dropped from the same height would hit Earth's surface at the same time if there was not any air resistance.

Word Watch

force a push or a pull

gravity force that pulls objects toward one another

mass amount of matter in an object, which is similar but not identical to weight

sphere round, three-dimensional object where all points on the surface are the same distance from the center

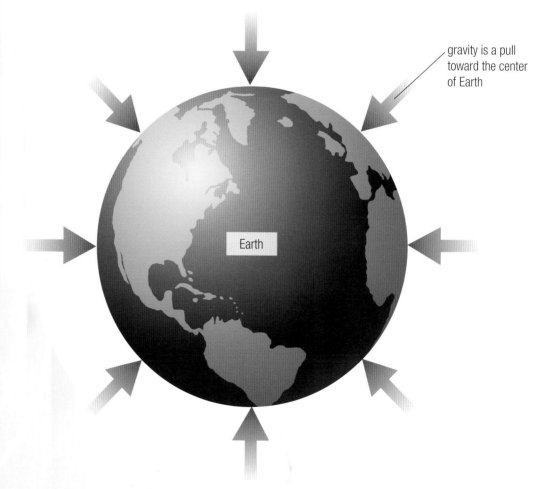

gravity is a pull toward the center of Earth

Earth

▲ Earth has a large gravitational pull that pulls us toward the ground.

Gravity and the Solar System

Gravity does not only exist on Earth. It exists all over the universe. Our solar system is a great example of gravity at work. When pushed or thrown, small objects travel in a parabola before falling to the ground, but the planets and moons in the solar system travel in a continuous **arc** (see diagram). There is something causing the planets to move in this way. That something is gravity. Gravitational pull causes moons to be attracted to planets and planets to be attracted to the sun.

Constant movement stops the planets and moons from smashing into the larger objects. The Moon is traveling fast enough to stop it crashing into Earth, but it is not moving fast enough or with enough force to free itself of Earth's gravitational pull. The same is true of Earth's movement in relation to the sun.

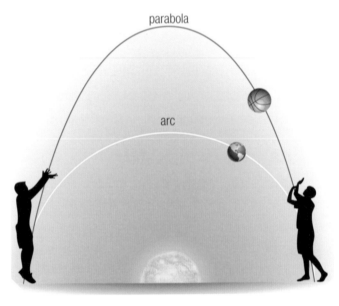

parabola

arc

◄ When a ball is thrown, it travels in a parabola shape through the air. The planets move in a continuous arc around the sun because of gravity.

Gravity, Weight, and Mass

Mass is the amount of matter in your body. Weight is the force of gravity on this mass. A person's mass stays the same wherever they are in the universe, but they would weigh different amounts on different planets because of the different gravitational pulls.

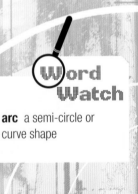

Word Watch

arc a semi-circle or curve shape

▼ Gravity causes the planets to move in constant paths around the sun.

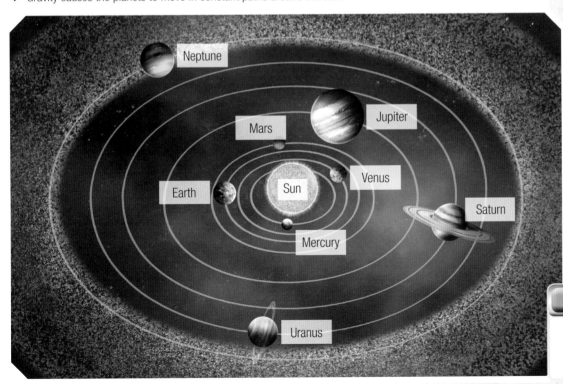

Neptune

Mars

Jupiter

Earth

Sun

Venus

Saturn

Mercury

Uranus

Web Watch ▼

www.historyforkids.org/
scienceforkids/physics/
space/gravity.htm

What Causes Tides?

Tides are caused by **gravity**. Most tides are caused by the gravitational pull between Earth and the Moon, although some types of tides also involve the sun.

The Pull of Gravity

As the Moon **orbits** Earth, Earth's gravity is pulling on the Moon. The Moon also has a gravitational **force**, but it is weaker than Earth's. The Moon is large enough to withstand a lot of Earth's pull, otherwise it would have crashed into Earth billions of years ago. The Moon is not large enough to withstand all the force, however, or it would speed away from Earth and not orbit it.

It is the smaller gravitational pull of the Moon on Earth that causes tides. As the Moon orbits Earth, the ocean that is on Earth's surface facing the Moon bulges outward, toward the Moon. The water **molecules** in the oceans move only a little bit toward the Moon because they are being pulled down at the same time by Earth's gravitational force. The part of the world that experiences this ocean bulge experiences a high tide, with higher water levels.

▼ The force of gravity does not pull just one way between Earth and the Moon, but Earth's gravitational pull is stronger because it is much larger.

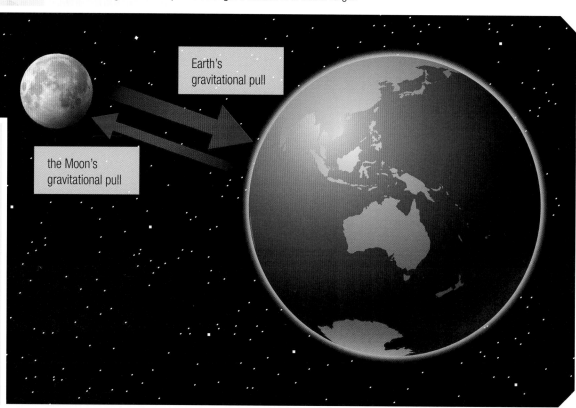

Earth's gravitational pull

the Moon's gravitational pull

Two Tides Each Day

The Moon travels around Earth once a day, but coastal areas on Earth experience two high tides a day. One tide occurs when an ocean is on the surface of Earth closest to the Moon, but what about the other high tide?

A second high tide occurs in the ocean at the point farthest from the Moon. This is because as the Moon's gravitational force pulls Earth very slightly toward the Moon, the ocean on the far side seems to bulge out a little bit and experiences a high tide, too.

The two areas of Earth that are at right angles to the Moon experience low tide. In these side positions, the gravitational pull from the Moon matches the pull of Earth.

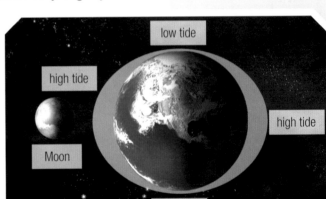

▶ Each coastal area experiences two high tides each day: once when the area is facing the Moon and once when it is facing away from the Moon. It also experiences two low tides each day.

What About the Sun?

The gravitational force of the Moon is largely responsible for the tides, but the sun also plays a role. When the Moon is directly between Earth and the sun and when Earth is directly between the Moon and the sun, the gravitational pull from the sun adds to the pull from the Moon making high tides higher then normal and low tides lower than normal. These tides are called spring tides.

When the sun and the Moon are **perpendicular** to each other in relation to Earth, their gravitational pulls from different directions cause weaker than normal tides. These are known as neap tides.

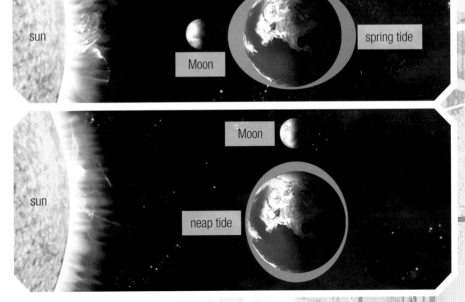

▲ The sun's gravitational pull sometimes works with and sometimes against the Moon's gravitational pull, causing spring tides and neap tides.

Web Watch ▼

oceanlink.island.net/oinfo/tides/tides.html
www.mos.org/oceans/motion/tides.html

From our view on Earth, an **eclipse** occurs when the sun, Earth, and Moon are all in a straight line. The order in which these bodies line up is different during a solar eclipse and a lunar eclipse.

Solar Eclipse

During a solar eclipse, the Moon passes between the sun and Earth. This has the effect of blocking the sunlight that can be seen from Earth and the Moon seems to cover the sun.

In most solar eclipses, the Moon does not completely cover the sun. The result is a bright ring of light around the outside of the Moon. These eclipses are known as annular eclipses.

Sometimes, the Moon completely blocks the view of the sun. In these cases, day turns into night for a few minutes. This is called a total eclipse.

Eclipse Blindness

Looking at the sun during a solar eclipse can result in eclipse blindness. Even though the sun is hidden from view, dangerous solar rays can burn a hole in the **retina** of the eye. People who want to watch an eclipse must take special precautions such as wearing special glasses.

Word Watch

eclipse when a planet, moon, or other body moves into the shadow of another

retina light-sensitive part of the eye that receives images and sends them to the brain

◄ A bright ring can be seen around the Moon in an annular solar eclipse.

▼ As the Moon moves in front of the sun, it blocks sunlight from reaching Earth.

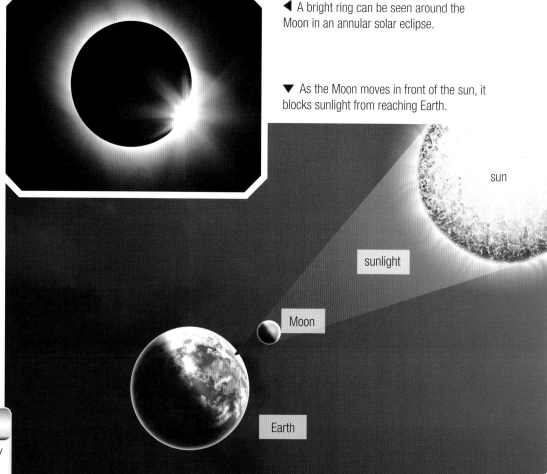

sun

sunlight

Moon

Earth

Web Watch ▼

www.space.com/eclipse/
www.mreclipse.com/
Special/LEprimer.html

Lunar Eclipse

During a lunar eclipse, the Moon passes into Earth's shadow and is blocked from the sun. A lunar eclipse can only occur when the Moon is in its full moon phase (see page 14).

During a partial lunar eclipse, part of the Moon is blocked from the sun and an area of darkness appears on the Moon. During a total lunar eclipse, the whole of the Moon is blocked from the sun. This has the effect of making the Moon appear reddish in color, because the only light that reaches the Moon has to pass through Earth's atmosphere, which filters out all the blue light and leaves only red or orange light.

▼ The whole of the Moon passes behind Earth during a total lunar eclipse. The light that reaches it makes it appear red.

▼ Only part of the Moon passes behind Earth during a partial lunar eclipse.

sunlight

sun

Moon

Earth

▲ As the Moon travels behind it, Earth blocks sunlight reaching the Moon.

Celestial Dragons and Angry Gods

Many ancient civilizations developed reasons for why eclipses occurred. The ancient Chinese believed that eclipses were caused by a **celestial** dragon trying to eat the sun or Moon. They banged drums during eclipses to frighten the dragon away. Other civilizations believed that an eclipse was a sign that the gods were angry or that some terrible event was about to occur.

Word Watch

celestial related to the sky or space

Index